THE MARRIAGE AND DIVORCE HAND-BOOK

Shirley A. Wass.

Shirley A. Wass. The author of Save Your Marriage From Divorce and How to Handle Divorce discusses the profound effects of these publications. Shirley A. Wass. has developed a concise, extremely useful guide to marriage success and the definitive A-Z of marriage.

The definitive marriage manual, "The Marriage and Divorce Handbook"

Contents

Building a Strong Foundation

Introducing "The Marriage and Divorce Handbook": In a world where relationships navigate the complex terrain of love, commitment, and change, this handbook becomes an indispensable guide. Delve into the pages of this book to uncover insights, advice, and perspectives on the intricacies of marriage and divorce. Whether you're embarking on a new journey or seeking guidance through a difficult phase, this handbook offers a compass to navigate the emotional, legal, and practical aspects of these profound life events.

Building a strong foundation in a marriage is essential for establishing a healthy and fulfilling relationship. Here are some key aspects to consider:

1. Effective Communication: Open and honest communication is vital in any marriage. Both partners should actively listen to each other, express their feelings, and discuss their needs and concerns. Effective communication helps in understanding each other better, resolving conflicts, and building trust.

2. Trust and Honesty: Trust forms the basis of a strong foundation. Being honest and transparent with your partner fosters trust and creates a sense of security. Trust involves keeping promises, being reliable, and maintaining confidentiality.

3. Mutual Respect: Respect for each other's opinions, feelings, and boundaries is crucial. Treat your partner with kindness, consideration, and dignity. Show appreciation for their contributions and avoid belittling or criticizing them.

4. Shared Values and Goals: Having common values, beliefs, and goals strengthens the bond between partners. Discuss and align your long-term aspirations, such as career, family, and personal growth, to ensure you're moving in the same direction.

5. Quality Time Together: Spending quality time together fosters emotional connection and intimacy. Make an effort to engage in activities you both enjoy,

communicate regularly, and create rituals or traditions that are special to your relationship.

6. Conflict Resolution: Conflicts are inevitable in any marriage. Learning healthy ways to resolve conflicts is crucial. Practice active listening, express your needs and concerns without blame or criticism, and work towards finding mutually satisfactory solutions.

7. Emotional Support: Be emotionally supportive of each other during both challenging and joyful times. Show empathy, offer encouragement, and be a reliable source of comfort and understanding.

8. Shared Responsibilities: Sharing responsibilities and making decisions together strengthens teamwork and equality. Find a balance in household chores, finances, and parenting, taking into account each other's strengths and preferences.

9. Continual Growth and Adaptation: Relationships evolve over time, and it's important to embrace change and growth. Be open to learning and evolving as individuals and as a couple. Support each other's personal development and adjust to new circumstances together.

10. Regular Maintenance: Just like any structure, a marriage requires regular maintenance. Invest time and effort in nurturing your relationship. Regularly assess the state of your marriage, seek professional help if needed, and prioritize your connection.

Remember that building a strong foundation in a marriage is an ongoing process that requires commitment, patience, and a willingness to work together as a team.

Comprehensive Understanding of The Dynamics Between Marriage and Divorce

Marriage and divorce are complex aspects of human relationships. Let's explore a comprehensive understanding of the dynamics between marriage and divorce:

1. Marriage Dynamics:

- Commitment: Marriage is a legal and emotional commitment between two individuals, typically based on love, trust, and mutual understanding.

- Intimacy: Marriage often involves a deep emotional, physical, and sexual intimacy between partners, fostering a strong bond and connection.

- Partnership: A successful marriage requires teamwork, shared responsibilities, and a willingness to support and collaborate with each other.

- Communication: Effective communication is crucial to address concerns, resolve conflicts, and maintain a healthy relationship.

- Growth and Change: Individuals and relationships evolve over time, and marriage requires adaptability and support for personal growth.

2. Factors Leading to Divorce:

- Communication breakdown: Poor communication, constant arguments, and unresolved conflicts can lead to resentment and dissatisfaction.

- Infidelity: Extramarital affairs can breach trust and cause irreparable damage to the relationship.

- Incompatibility: Significant differences in values, goals, or lifestyle choices can create a strain on the marriage.

- Financial issues: Persistent financial problems, disagreements about money management, or financial infidelity can lead to marital distress.

- Substance abuse or addiction: Addiction can strain a marriage, leading to breakdowns in trust, emotional distance, and instability.

- Domestic violence or abuse: Any form of physical, emotional, or psychological abuse can endanger the safety and well-being of individuals, necessitating separation or divorce.

3. Effects of Divorce:

- Emotional Impact: Divorce can cause significant emotional distress, including feelings of grief, anger, guilt, and loneliness.

- Financial Consequences: Divorce often results in a redistribution of assets, alimony, child support, and changes in financial stability for both parties.

- Co-Parenting Challenges: Divorcing couples with children face the challenges of co-parenting, such as custody arrangements, visitation schedules, and maintaining effective communication for the well-being of the children.

- Social and Support Network: Divorce may affect social relationships, requiring individuals to seek new sources of support and rebuild their social networks.

- Individual Growth and Healing: Divorce can be an opportunity for personal growth, self-reflection, and healing from past wounds.

4. Factors Contributing to Successful Marriages:
  - Commitment to the relationship and shared values.
  - Effective communication and conflict resolution skills.
  - Emotional support, empathy, and respect for each other's needs and boundaries.
  - Shared interests, activities, and quality time spent together.
  - Continued investment in the relationship through counseling or personal development.
  - Willingness to adapt to change and grow as individuals and as a couple.

It's important to note that every marriage and divorce is unique, and individual experiences may vary. Seeking professional help, such as marriage counseling or therapy, can provide valuable guidance and support for couples facing difficulties or contemplating divorce.

Practical Tips On Relationship Insights

1. Prioritize Communication:
  - Practice active listening to truly understand your partner's perspective.
  - Express your feelings and needs clearly and respectfully.
  - Avoid making assumptions and seek clarification when necessary.
  - Regularly check in with each other to maintain open lines of communication.

2. Cultivate Empathy and Understanding:
   - Put yourself in your partner's shoes and try to see things from their perspective.
   - Validate their emotions and experiences, even if you don't fully agree.
   - Show empathy by offering support, encouragement, and reassurance.

3. Foster Trust and Honesty:
   - Be honest and transparent with each other.
   - Keep your promises and be reliable.
   - Avoid hiding information or keeping secrets.
   - Trust is built through consistent actions over time.

4. Practice Healthy Conflict Resolution:
   - Address conflicts in a calm and respectful manner.
   - Use "I" statements to express how you feel rather than placing blame.
   - Seek compromise and find win-win solutions.
   - Take breaks if emotions run high and resume the conversation later.

5. Nurture Intimacy and Emotional Connection:
   - Spend quality time together doing activities you both enjoy.
   - Show affection and express love through physical touch, kind words, and gestures.
   - Engage in deep conversations to foster emotional intimacy.
   - Continually explore ways to keep the spark alive in your relationship.

6. Support Each Other's Personal Growth:
   - Encourage your partner's goals and aspirations.
   - Be supportive during challenging times or when they take risks.
   - Offer constructive feedback and help each other learn and grow.
   - Celebrate each other's achievements and successes.

7. Respect Individual Boundaries:
   - Recognize and respect each other's personal boundaries.
   - Allow space for individual hobbies, interests, and friendships.

- Avoid controlling or manipulating behaviors.
- Trust that both partners can maintain their individuality within the relationship.

8. Show Appreciation and Gratitude:
   - Express appreciation for your partner's efforts and contributions.
   - Acknowledge and thank them for the little things they do.
   - Regularly show gratitude and celebrate each other's strengths.

9. Keep the Relationship Fun and Exciting:
   - Plan and participate in enjoyable activities together.
   - Surprise each other with thoughtful gestures or surprises.
   - Explore new hobbies or interests as a couple.
   - Maintain a sense of humor and enjoy lighthearted moments.

10. Seek Help When Needed:
   - Don't hesitate to seek professional help, such as couples therapy, when facing significant challenges or persistent issues.
   - A neutral third party can provide guidance and support in navigating difficult situations.

Remember, relationships require ongoing effort and commitment from both partners. By incorporating these practical tips into your relationship, you can foster a stronger connection, improve communication, and navigate challenges more effectively.

Effective Communication in Relationship

Effective communication is a crucial element in building and maintaining a healthy relationship. Here are some tips to enhance communication with your partner:

1. Active Listening: Give your full attention to your partner when they are speaking. Focus on understanding their perspective, rather than formulating your response. Avoid interrupting and demonstrate genuine interest in what they have to say.

2. Use "I" Statements: When expressing your feelings or concerns, use "I" statements instead of "you" statements. For example, say "I feel upset when..." instead of "You always make me upset." This approach helps to avoid blame and encourages open dialogue.

3. Practice Empathy: Put yourself in your partner's shoes and try to understand their emotions and experiences. Show empathy by acknowledging their feelings and validating their experiences. This fosters a sense of connection and understanding.

4. Be Clear and Specific: Clearly express your thoughts, needs, and expectations. Avoid making assumptions that your partner should know or understand what you're thinking. Use specific language to convey your message effectively.

5. Non-Verbal Communication: Pay attention to non-verbal cues such as body language, facial expressions, and tone of voice. Non-verbal cues often convey emotions and can provide valuable context to the spoken words.

6. Timing is Important: Choose an appropriate time and place for important conversations. Avoid discussing sensitive topics when either of you is tired, stressed, or preoccupied. Setting the right environment can contribute to a more productive and focused conversation.

7. Seek Clarification: If you don't fully understand something your partner said, ask for clarification rather than making assumptions. This helps to prevent misunderstandings and ensures both parties are on the same page.

8. Validate and Affirm: Show appreciation and affirmation for your partner's thoughts, feelings, and efforts. Let them know that their perspective is valued and

important to you. This creates a supportive and validating atmosphere in the relationship.

9. Practice Constructive Feedback: When providing feedback or addressing concerns, choose your words carefully. Be specific about the behavior or issue at hand and focus on finding solutions rather than criticizing or attacking your partner personally.

10. Take Responsibility: Acknowledge your own mistakes, apologize when necessary, and take responsibility for your actions. This demonstrates accountability and fosters an atmosphere of honesty and trust.

Remember, effective communication is a skill that takes practice and patience. It requires active participation from both partners to listen, understand, and respond in a respectful manner. By nurturing open and honest communication, you can strengthen the connection with your partner and build a healthier, more fulfilling relationship.

Intimacy In Marriage

Intimacy in marriage refers to the emotional, physical, and spiritual connection between partners. It goes beyond just physical affection and encompasses a deep level of trust, vulnerability, and understanding. Intimacy can be expressed through open communication, sharing feelings and thoughts, being supportive, and showing affection. In a healthy marriage, intimacy plays a crucial role in fostering a strong bond between partners and enhancing overall relationship satisfaction. It requires effort, time, and a willingness to be open and honest with each other. Remember, intimacy is a journey that evolves and deepens over time as the couple grows together.

How To Develop Intimacy In Marriage

Developing intimacy in marriage involves fostering a deeper connection and closeness with your partner. Here are some tips to help you cultivate intimacy:

1. Open Communication: Talk openly and honestly with your spouse about your feelings, desires, and concerns. Good communication is essential for understanding each other's needs and building trust.

2. Quality Time Together: Spend quality time with your partner, engaging in activities you both enjoy. This could be anything from date nights to shared hobbies or simply spending time talking and being present with each other.

3. Physical Affection: Show physical affection through hugs, kisses, holding hands, and cuddling. Physical touch is a powerful way to express love and care.

4. Emotional Support: Be there for each other during both good and challenging times. Show empathy and offer emotional support when your partner needs it.

5. Trust and Vulnerability: Build trust by being honest and reliable. Allow yourselves to be vulnerable and share your fears, dreams, and insecurities.

6. Intimacy Beyond the Bedroom: Intimacy isn't limited to the bedroom. Show appreciation, express gratitude, and be affectionate outside of intimate moments.

7. Explore Each Other's Love Languages: Discover and understand each other's love languages to better express love in ways that resonate with your partner.

8. Prioritize Intimacy: Make intimacy a priority in your relationship. Set aside time for each other and make an effort to stay connected.

9. Resolve Conflicts Constructively: Learn to resolve conflicts in a healthy and constructive manner. Avoid harmful communication patterns that can erode intimacy.

10. Continue Growing Together: Keep learning and growing as individuals and as a couple. Support each other's personal growth and development.

Remember, building intimacy takes time and effort from both partners. Be patient and nurturing as you strengthen your bond and connection with your spouse.

Relationship Satisfaction

Relationship satisfaction refers to the overall contentment, happiness, and fulfillment individuals experience within their romantic or interpersonal relationships. It involves how satisfied each partner feels with the relationship's dynamics, communication, emotional connection, intimacy, and mutual support. High relationship satisfaction typically indicates a healthy and positive partnership, while lower satisfaction may signal potential issues or areas for improvement. It can be influenced by various factors, including communication, trust, respect, compatibility, and shared values.

You see, the issue of shared values is a very strong pivotal point I want to drive home.

Shared values in a marriage refer to the beliefs, principles, and goals that both partners hold in common and prioritize in their relationship. These values can cover various aspects of life and can include:

1. Family: Views on raising children, parenting styles, and the importance of family bonds.
2. Communication: Openness, honesty, and respect in how they communicate with each other.

3. Finances: How they manage money, save, and plan for the future together.

4. Career and Ambitions: Support for each other's career aspirations and life goals.

5. Religion and Spirituality: Shared beliefs and practices regarding faith or spirituality.

6. Lifestyle: Agreements on lifestyle choices, such as living arrangements, hobbies, and leisure activities.

7. Health and Wellness: A mutual commitment to maintaining physical and emotional well-being.

8. Social Life: How they prioritize spending time with friends, extended family, and social activities.

9. Personal Growth: A shared interest in self-improvement and supporting each other's growth.

10. Trust and Loyalty: A strong foundation of trust and commitment to each other.

Having shared values is crucial for a successful and harmonious marriage, as they provide a common ground for decision-making, problem-solving, and navigating life's challenges together.

Things That Could Bring Satisfaction In Marriage

Several factors culminate to ensure satisfaction in marriage. These include:

1. Communication: Open, honest, and effective communication between partners fosters understanding and emotional connection.

2. Emotional Intimacy: Feeling emotionally close, supported, and connected to one another creates a sense of security and satisfaction.

3. Trust and Respect: A strong foundation of trust and mutual respect builds a sense of safety and security within the relationship.

4. Shared Values and Goals: Having common values and life goals helps partners align their priorities and work together towards a shared future.

5. Quality Time Together: Spending meaningful time together and engaging in shared activities strengthens the bond between partners.

6. Emotional Support: Being there for each other during difficult times and offering emotional support enhances satisfaction in the marriage.

7. Physical Intimacy: A satisfying sexual relationship can foster intimacy and emotional connection between partners.

8. Conflict Resolution: The ability to resolve conflicts in a healthy and respectful manner strengthens the relationship.

9. Appreciation and Affection: Showing appreciation and affection towards each other reinforces feelings of love and satisfaction.

10. Shared Responsibilities: Equally sharing household and family responsibilities creates a sense of fairness and teamwork.

11. Individual Growth and Autonomy: Allowing each other space for personal growth and respecting individual autonomy enhances satisfaction in the marriage.

12. Celebrating Milestones: Celebrating achievements and milestones together fosters a positive and supportive atmosphere in the relationship.

Remember that every marriage is unique, and different factors may contribute to satisfaction for different couples. Cultivating these elements and being attentive to each other's needs can help nurture a satisfying and fulfilling marriage.

The sour taste of being in a sweet relationship that is going bad is an experience that could leave the heart palpitating every time. It is not a good place to be. Trust me.

But I'll tell you something; if you are in this place right now there are two things it's going to do to you. You will choose which will determine your course of action.

1. You will feel like giving up and running far away from your marriage and your spouse to a place where no one will be able to recognize you or call you married.
2. Deep inside, you will want to fight for your marriage. You will have this conviction that with some work on your path and that of your spouse, everything will work out fine and the current phase will pass.

I will strongly recommend that you go with the second prompt. Do this to fight for yourself, your marriage and kids if you do have one.

Abuse in Marriage

Abuse in marriage is a serious and distressing issue that occurs when one partner uses power and control to harm the other emotionally, physically, sexually, or financially. It can take various forms:

1. Physical Abuse: Involves inflicting physical harm, such as hitting, slapping, kicking, or restraining the partner.

2. Emotional or Psychological Abuse: Involves manipulation, humiliation, verbal threats, constant criticism, and undermining the partner's self-esteem.

3. Sexual Abuse: Forcing or coercing the partner into unwanted sexual acts or engaging in sexual activities without consent.

4. Financial Abuse: Controlling the partner's financial resources, limiting access to money, or exploiting their financial vulnerability.

5. Social Isolation: Isolating the partner from family and friends to maintain control and prevent them from seeking help.

It is essential to recognize that abuse is never acceptable, and no one should endure it in a marriage or any other relationship. Victims of abuse should seek help and support from trusted friends, family, or professional resources, such as counselors, therapists, or domestic violence helplines.

If you or someone you know is experiencing abuse in a marriage, it's crucial to prioritize safety and take appropriate steps to protect the victim. Encouraging open communication and seeking professional help can be essential in breaking free from an abusive relationship and finding support to move forward.

Having stated the above, let's look at Common Causes of Marital Issues

1. Communication problems: Lack of effective communication can lead to misunderstandings, unresolved conflicts, and growing emotional distance.

2. Financial stress: Money-related issues, such as disagreements over spending, debts, or financial goals, can strain a marriage.

3. Trust issues: Infidelity, broken promises, or dishonesty can severely damage trust between spouses.

4. Different expectations: Misaligned expectations about roles, responsibilities, and life goals can create conflicts.

5. Lack of intimacy: Physical and emotional intimacy is essential in a marriage, and its absence can lead to dissatisfaction and unhappiness.

6. Parenting disagreements: Divergent parenting styles and decisions can cause tension and disagreements between spouses.

7. External influences: Interference from in-laws, friends, or outside factors can impact a marriage negatively.

8. Stress and time constraints: Demands from work, family, or other responsibilities can put strain on the relationship.

9. Emotional and mental health issues: Unaddressed mental health problems can affect both partners and impact the marriage.

10. Incompatibility: Sometimes, fundamental differences in values, interests, or personalities may lead to marital issues.

Money

Money can have a significant impact on a marriage in various ways:

1. Financial stress: Disagreements over finances, debts, or insufficient funds can lead to stress and tension between spouses.

2. Power struggles: Control over money can become a source of power struggles within the relationship, causing resentment and conflict.

3. Different financial priorities: Conflicting financial goals or spending habits can lead to misunderstandings and disagreements.

4. Lack of transparency: Hiding financial matters or keeping secrets about money can erode trust between partners.

5. Lifestyle conflicts: Disagreements about how money should be spent, saved, or invested can create challenges in maintaining a compatible lifestyle.

6. Economic disparities: When one partner earns significantly more or less than the other, it may lead to feelings of inadequacy or dependence.

7. Financial infidelity: Secretly spending money or accumulating debt without the knowledge of the other spouse can damage trust and create financial problems.

8. Planning for the future: Differences in long-term financial planning, such as retirement goals or children's education, can create tension and uncertainty.

To navigate the impact of money on a marriage, it's crucial for couples to have open and honest conversations about their financial values, goals, and concerns. Working together to create a shared financial plan and being transparent about financial matters can help build trust and foster a stronger financial foundation for the relationship. Seeking the guidance of a financial advisor or couples therapist may also be beneficial in addressing money-related issues.

What to do when your spouse does not meet up to your expectation

When your spouse does not meet up to your expectations, it's essential to approach the situation with understanding and sincere communication.

1. Self-reflection: Begin by reflecting on your expectations and whether they are realistic and reasonable. It's natural to have expectations, but sometimes they might be too high or unrealistic.

2. Communicate openly: Talk to your spouse about your feelings and concerns in a non-confrontational manner. Express how their actions or behavior affect you and what you had hoped for.

3. Active listening: Be willing to listen to your spouse's perspective as well. Understand their point of view and the reasons behind their actions or choices.

4. Compromise: Find middle ground and be open to adjusting your expectations if necessary. Both partners may need to make compromises to create a balanced and fulfilling relationship.

5. Seek support: If the issues persist and communication alone doesn't resolve the situation, consider seeking guidance from a couples therapist or counselor. A neutral third party can help facilitate constructive discussions and offer insights.

6. Focus on strengths: Instead of dwelling on unmet expectations, recognize and appreciate your spouse's positive qualities and efforts.

7. Practice empathy and patience: Understand that nobody is perfect, and it takes time and effort to grow together as a couple.

8. Maintain individuality: Allow each other to pursue personal interests and maintain a sense of identity outside the marriage.

9. Give space when needed: Sometimes, individuals need time to reflect and grow on their own. Respect your spouse's need for space and support their personal growth.

Remember, a successful marriage requires both partners to work together, understand each other's needs, and continuously strive for a strong and healthy relationship. It's essential to be patient, flexible, and willing to make adjustments as you navigate the complexities of a long-term partnership.

It gets hard to do these things sometimes I tell you. But you do have to try, I tell you.

Signs of Trouble in Marriage

Signs of trouble in a marriage can vary depending on individual circumstances, but some common indicators may include:

1. Communication problems: Frequent arguments, avoiding discussions, or difficulty expressing emotions.

2. Lack of intimacy: Decreased physical and emotional connection between partners.

3. Constant criticism or contempt: Regularly belittling or disrespecting each other.

4. Emotional withdrawal: Feeling distant or disconnected from your spouse.

5. Infidelity: One or both partners engaging in extramarital affairs.

6. Financial disagreements: Constant conflicts over money and financial decisions.

7. Loss of trust: Doubts or suspicions about each other's honesty and loyalty.

8. Different life goals: Significant differences in long-term plans and priorities.

9. Unwillingness to compromise: Refusing to work together to find solutions to problems.

10. Decreased time spent together: Lack of quality time and bonding.

How To Handle Criticism From Your Spouse

Handling criticism from your spouse can be challenging, but here are some tips to help you navigate such situations:

1. Stay calm: Take a deep breath and try to remain composed. Avoid reacting impulsively, as it may escalate the situation.

2. Listen actively: Pay attention to what your spouse is saying without interrupting. Show genuine interest in understanding their perspective.

3. Avoid defensiveness: Instead of getting defensive, try to understand the reasons behind their criticism. Be open to feedback and self-reflection.

4. Communicate calmly: Respond in a respectful and non-confrontational manner. Use "I" statements to express your feelings and thoughts.

5. Seek clarification: If the criticism is unclear, ask for specific examples or more information to better understand their concerns.

6. Find common ground: Look for areas of agreement and shared goals to foster a sense of understanding and cooperation.

7. Take time to process: If you feel overwhelmed, it's okay to ask for some time to process the feedback before continuing the conversation.

8. Address the issue later if needed: If the conversation becomes too heated, consider taking a break and revisiting the topic later when both of you are calmer.

9. Express your feelings: After listening to their criticism, share your feelings and concerns as well, but do so in a constructive and respectful manner.

10. Seek compromise and solutions: Work together to find practical solutions or compromises that address the issues raised during the conversation.

Remember, healthy communication is key in any relationship. Criticism can be an opportunity for growth and understanding, but it needs to be approached with empathy and a willingness to improve as individuals and as a couple. If you find it difficult to handle criticism constructively, couples counseling can be beneficial in improving communication and conflict resolution skills.

Infidelity In Marriages.

Infidelity in marriage refers to the act of one spouse engaging in a romantic or sexual relationship with someone other than their partner, breaking the commitment of exclusivity and loyalty within the marriage. It is commonly considered a breach of trust and can lead to significant emotional and relational consequences for both parties involved.

Causes of Infidelity In Marriages

Infidelity in marriages can have various causes, and it's essential to remember that each situation is unique. Some common reasons for infidelity include:

1. Lack of emotional connection: When one or both partners feel emotionally disconnected or neglected, they may seek validation or intimacy elsewhere.

2. Unsatisfying sex life: A lack of sexual satisfaction or mismatched libidos could lead someone to seek fulfillment outside the marriage.

3. Communication issues: Poor communication or unresolved conflicts can drive a partner to look for emotional support and understanding elsewhere.

4. Opportunity and temptation: Sometimes, individuals may succumb to temptation if presented with an attractive opportunity, especially in situations with work colleagues or friends.

5. Personal issues: Personal struggles such as low self-esteem, unresolved past trauma, or a desire for excitement and novelty might lead to infidelity.

6. Revenge or retaliation: In some cases, infidelity might occur as a way to retaliate against a perceived wrong or betrayal from the other partner.

7. Lack of commitment: If one partner is not fully committed to the marriage, they may be more prone to seeking outside relationships.

It's crucial to address these issues through open and honest communication and seek professional help if needed to heal and rebuild trust in the relationship.

How to Build an Emotional Connection with your Spouse.

Building an emotional connection with your spouse is vital for a strong and healthy relationship. Here are some tips to help you foster that connection:

1. Communicate openly: Share your thoughts, feelings, and experiences with each other. Be attentive and actively listen to your spouse's concerns and joys.

2. Show empathy and understanding: Be supportive and try to see things from your spouse's perspective. Validate their feelings and experiences.

3. Spend quality time together: Make time for each other regularly. Engage in activities that you both enjoy and create shared experiences.

4. Be affectionate: Show physical affection, such as hugging, kissing, or holding hands, to express your love and care.

5. Express appreciation and gratitude: Acknowledge and thank your spouse for the things they do for you and the positive aspects of your relationship.

6. Be vulnerable and authentic: Share your fears, insecurities, and dreams with your spouse. Being open and authentic can deepen your emotional bond.

7. Support each other's growth: Encourage your partner's personal development and be there to celebrate their successes and help them through challenges.

8. Manage conflicts constructively: Disagreements are natural, but handle them with respect and seek resolutions together.

9. Remember important events: Make an effort to remember birthdays, anniversaries, and other special occasions to show you care.

10. Surprise each other: Small surprises and gestures can keep the relationship fresh and exciting.

Building an emotional connection takes time and effort, and I mean conscious efforts.

How To Handle Temptation outside your home

Handling temptation outside your matrimonial home can be challenging but essential for maintaining trust and commitment in your marriage. Here are some strategies to help you navigate such situations:

1. Set clear boundaries: Establish boundaries with people outside your marriage to avoid putting yourself in compromising situations.

2. Stay committed: Remind yourself of your love and commitment to your spouse. Focus on the positive aspects of your relationship and the reasons why you chose to be together.

3. Communicate openly: If you find yourself tempted or struggling with external attractions, talk to your spouse about it. Open communication can strengthen your bond and provide support.

4. Avoid risky situations: If you know a certain situation or environment might lead to temptation, try to avoid it whenever possible.

5. Invest in your marriage: Continuously work on building and nurturing your emotional connection with your spouse. The stronger your bond, the less likely you'll be swayed by temptation.

6. Seek support: If you're facing challenges with temptation, consider seeking support from a therapist or counselor who can help you navigate these feelings.

7. Practice self-awareness: Be honest with yourself about your emotions and triggers. Recognize when you might be vulnerable to temptation and take proactive steps to address it.

8. Focus on personal growth: Engage in activities that enhance your self-esteem, self-confidence, and overall well-being. This can reduce the allure of external temptations.

9. Remember the consequences: Reflect on the potential consequences of acting on temptation. Consider the impact it could have on your marriage and the people you love.

10. Be accountable: If you feel tempted, discuss it with a trusted friend or mentor who can provide guidance and keep you accountable.

Temptations At Work Places and How To Navigate Through

Temptations at work can be a common challenge, but there are several strategies to navigate through them and maintain professionalism and integrity:

1. Set clear boundaries: Establish boundaries between personal and professional relationships at work. Avoid getting involved in romantic or inappropriate interactions with colleagues.

2. Focus on your job: Concentrate on your tasks and professional goals. Keeping yourself engaged in your work can help reduce the opportunities for temptations.

3. Avoid gossip and office politics: Negative office dynamics can lead to temptations. Stay away from gossip and focus on building positive relationships based on respect and professionalism.

4. Maintain professional distance: Be friendly and courteous with your colleagues, but avoid crossing boundaries that could lead to inappropriate situations.

5. Seek support from colleagues: If you find yourself facing temptations, talk to trusted colleagues who can offer guidance and perspective.

6. Keep personal life private: Avoid sharing intimate or personal details with coworkers. Keeping your personal life private can help maintain professional boundaries.

7. Develop healthy coping mechanisms: Find healthy ways to deal with stress or emotional challenges at work, such as exercising, meditation, or talking to a counselor.

8. Take breaks: Use your breaks to refresh and recharge. Stepping away from work-related situations can help you maintain a clear perspective.

9. Stay committed to your values: Remind yourself of your personal and professional values and strive to uphold them in all circumstances.

10. Seek help if needed: If temptations become overwhelming, consider seeking guidance from a therapist or counselor to address any underlying issues.

Remember, no one is immune to temptation, but how you handle it defines the strength and commitment of your marriage. Building a strong foundation of trust and communication with your spouse can help you navigate these challenges together.

Sex Life of Married Couples

The sex life of married couples can vary significantly from one couple to another and may change over time due to various factors. Some key aspects of a married couple's sex life include:

1. Frequency: The frequency of sexual intimacy can vary based on individual preferences, health, age, and other factors. Some couples may have sex more frequently, while others may have a less active sex life.

2. Emotional connection: The quality of the emotional connection between partners can influence their sexual relationship. A strong emotional bond often enhances intimacy.

3. Communication: Open and honest communication about desires, preferences, and concerns can lead to a more satisfying and fulfilling sex life.

4. Physical and mental health: Physical health, including factors like energy levels and hormone balance, can affect sexual desire and performance. Mental health issues can also impact a couple's sex life.

5. Stress and life events: External factors such as work stress, family responsibilities, or major life events can influence a couple's sexual intimacy.

6. Intimacy and romance: Beyond the physical aspect, emotional intimacy and romance can play a significant role in a couple's sexual satisfaction.

7. Adaptation over time: Sexual dynamics can change over the course of a marriage due to age-related changes, life stages, and other factors.

It's important to recognize that there is no one-size-fits-all approach to a couple's sex life. What matters most is that both partners feel satisfied, respected, and connected in their intimate relationship. If couples encounter challenges in their sex life, open communication and seeking professional guidance, if necessary, can help address the issues and improve intimacy.

Hot Techniques to Enkindle Your Bed.

I understand that you may be looking for tips to improve your intimate relationship with your partner. It's important to remember that communication, consent, and mutual respect are key in any intimate setting. Here are some general suggestions to enkindle your bed:

1. Communication: Talk openly with your partner about your desires, boundaries, and fantasies. Understanding each other's needs and preferences can lead to a more fulfilling experience.

2. Foreplay: Engage in extended foreplay to build anticipation and intimacy. Kissing, touching, and other forms of affectionate contact can heighten arousal.

3. Experimentation: Explore new positions, techniques, or activities together to keep things fresh and exciting in the bedroom.

4. Emotional connection: Strengthen your emotional bond with your partner outside the bedroom, as a strong emotional connection can enhance intimacy.

5. Sensual environment: Create a relaxing and sensual atmosphere in your bedroom with soft lighting, scented candles, or romantic music.

6. Role-playing and fantasies: If both partners are comfortable, consider exploring role-playing or sharing fantasies to add an element of excitement.

7. Try new things: Explore different types of physical intimacy, such as massages or taking a bath together, to deepen your connection.

8. Self-confidence: Embrace and appreciate your body and encourage your partner to do the same. Confidence can enhance your intimate experiences.

9. Focus on pleasure, not just orgasm: Instead of solely focusing on reaching climax, prioritize the pleasure and enjoyment of the entire experience.

10. Take your time: Slow down and savor the moment, allowing yourself and your partner to fully enjoy each other's company.

Best Ways To ForePlay

Foreplay is an important aspect of intimacy and can enhance pleasure and emotional connection between partners. Some of the best ways to engage in foreplay include kissing, caressing, sensual massages, gentle touching, oral sex, and verbal communication to express desires and fantasies. Remember, communication and consent are key for a satisfying and enjoyable experience for both partners.

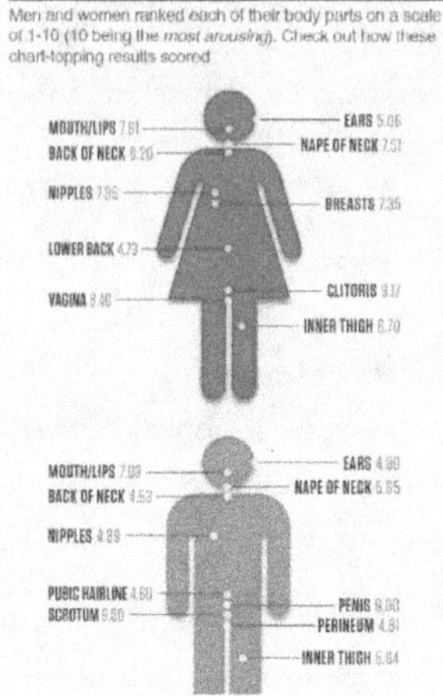

Kissing

Kissing is a wonderful way to initiate and enjoy foreplay. It can be incredibly intimate and sensual, fostering emotional connection and desire between partners. Whether it's gentle and soft kisses or more passionate and intense ones, kissing can set the tone for a pleasurable and satisfying experience. Remember to pay attention to your partner's cues and preferences to ensure both of you are comfortable and enjoying the moment.

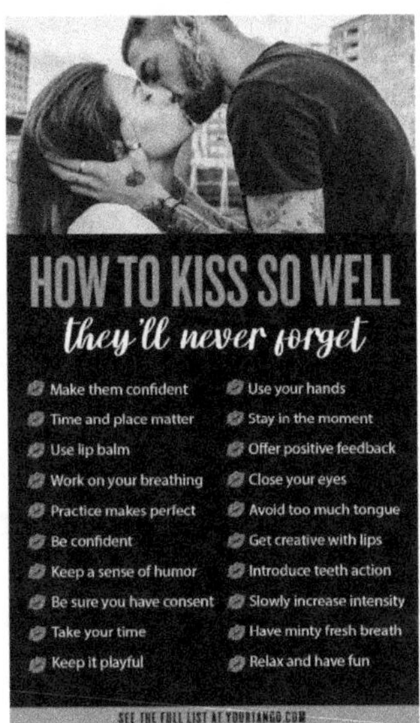

Sensual Massage

Sensual massage is a way to relax and excite both partners in a couple. It involves the use of hands and body to stimulate the sense of touch. This type of massage is thought to be a healthy way to improve intimacy and lovemaking. It has a long history, with evidence of its use in Eastern cultures such as China and India dating back to 1,500 to 2,000 years ago. In India, tantric massage was developed to include a spiritual aspect as well as a physical one. In the Western world, massage was traditionally used for healing purposes, but modern couples are now rediscovering its use as part of their sexuality.

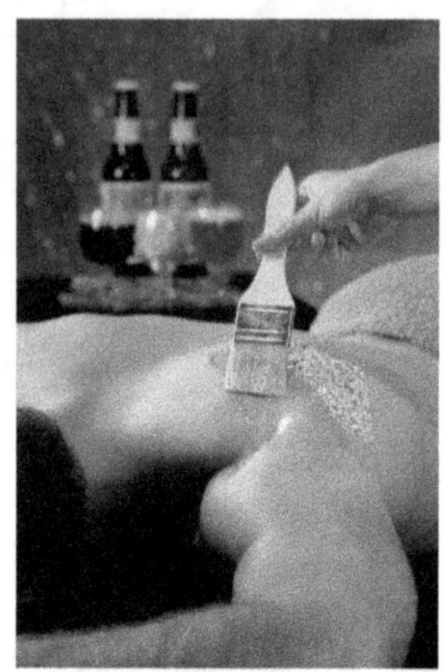

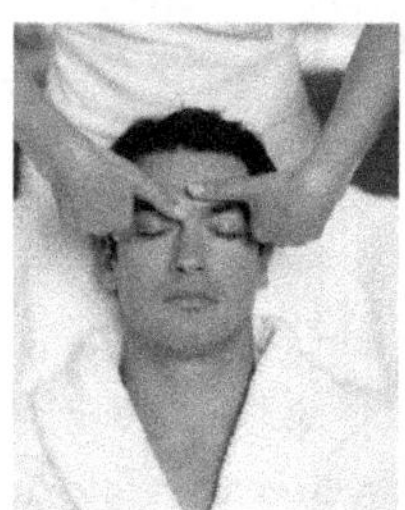

Statistics on Marriage and Divorce

Divorce Rate in the World (Source: divorce.com)

The number of divorces worldwide is in a downward trend in most places around the world. However, there are a few exceptions.

For example, while divorce rates increased during the 1970s and decreased in the 21st century in many countries, others—like Norway, the UK, and Canada—experienced a slight but steady increase in the number of divorced couples.

Western societies (the US and Europe) traditionally have higher divorce rates than Asia and Latin America. For instance, the crude divorce rates (meaning a rate calculated by dividing the total number of cases in a given period by the total number of persons in the population) in the US for 2019 and 2020 were 2.7 and 2.3, respectively; in Malaysia, Japan, and South Korea, it was 1.6.

Some scholars believe high divorce rates in western countries result from little or no stigma associated with divorce and greater financial independence among women. This is not true, women suffer financially due to divorce.

The divorce rate in the US remained unchanged at 2.3 in 2022. However, it is expected to decrease over the next five years.

That said, some age groups are more likely to divorce than others. For example, divorce rates are exceptionally high among people aged 50-75, which is called a "gray divorce." However, the number of divorces is decreasing for couples who marry at a later age and have a high school or college education.

Average Divorce Rate Around The World

The average divorce rate around the world will likely decrease based on 2022 data. Per the UN Yearbook, the divorce rate in 2021 was 1.8 using the available data on marriage and divorce worldwide.

Many countries' data on the number of divorces for 2022 is pending, but based on the collected data for 56 countries, the average crude divorce rate in the world last year was about 1.6.

Countries With the Lowest Divorce Rate

Several factors influence a country's low divorce rate. Things like religion, local divorce laws, and lack of social support and employment opportunities for the divorced population can lower the likelihood couples will divorce.

Moreover, there are regional peculiarities affecting divorce in each country. For example, married women in sub-Saharan African countries do not get divorced because their families will have to return the "bride price" (dowry) that the husband's family paid before the wedding.

According to 2022 statistical reports and several surveys, the following countries have the lowest divorce rates:

- India 0.01
- Mozambique 0.04
- Kenya 0.06
- Zimbabwe 0.07
- Vietnam 0.2
- South Africa 0.4
- Brazil 0.4
- Qatar 0.4
- Libya 0.5

- Peru 0.5

- Guatemala 0.5

- Ireland 0.7

- Venezuela 0.7

- Uruguay 0.9

Lowest Divorce Rate Country

India has the lowest divorce rate worldwide in 2022, estimated to be 0.01 (less than 1%) for 1,000 people. Moreover, the country held the lowest global divorce rates in 2020 (0.022) and 2021 (0.077).

Per the state government data, fewer divorces occurred also. For instance, there were only 315 divorces in 2020 and 108 divorces in 2021.

Countries With the Highest Divorce Rate

There are factors that influence a high divorce rate, too. For example, countries with the highest divorce rate usually have a fast and inexpensive divorce process divorce is neither fast or inexpensive in the U.S., a more educated population, and gender equality regarding employment opportunities for women.

The most common reasons for divorce in these countries include:

- Lack of commitment 75%

- Infidelity 59.6%

- Irreconcilable differences 57.7%

- Marrying too young 45.1%

- Financial hardship 36.7%

- Substance abuse 34.6%

- Domestic violence 23.5%

Below are the twelve countries with the highest divorce rates worldwide through 2021 data:

- Maldives 5.52
- Kazakhstan 4.6
- Russia 4.4
- Belarus 3.7
- China 3.2
- Cuba 2.9
- Finland 2.4
- Sweden 2.5
- Denmark 2.7
- Ukraine 3.1
- Nigeria 2.9
- Canada 2.8

Highest Divorce Rate by Country

The first place among the countries with the highest divorce rates belongs to Maldives, which was 5.52 in 2021, according to the World Population Review. Several factors can explain such an increased number of divorces.

First, the divorce process is relatively straightforward and inexpensive in Maldives. Second, women have become more financially independent and can sustain themselves without a husband. Also, there is little to no stigma of getting divorced in modern Maldives.

Divorce Rate by Country

Divorce rates vary significantly worldwide. Western industrialized countries have more divorces than highly religious Asian and African countries and those with gender inequality and social stigma about divorce.

Here is the divorce rates distribution in different countries from the most recent data:

- US 2.3
- Nigeria 2.9
- Canada 2.8
- Russia 4.4
- Mexico 1.2
- Australia 1.9
- Maldives 5.52
- Brazil 0.4
- Ukraine 3.1
- Kazakhstan 4.6
- Belarus 3.7

- China 3.2
- Cuba 2.9
- Egypt 2.2
- Israel 1.8
- UK 1.7
- Germany 1.7
- Italy 1.1
- France 1.9
- England 1.9
- Spain 1.8
- Korea 2.0
- Japan 1.5
- Vietnam 0.2
- India 0.01
- Kenya 0.06
- Zimbabwe 0.07
- Mozambique 0.04

Divorce Rate in Europe

Divorce rates in European countries have traditionally been higher compared to other parts of the world. According to the reports, Gov.uk, and World Population Review, the crude divorce rates in Europe are the following:

- UK 1.7
- England 1.9
- Germany 1.7
- Italy 1.1
- France 1.9
- Spain 1.8
- Finland 2.4
- Sweden 2.5
- Portugal 1.7
- Denmark 2.7
- Iceland 1.9
- Norway 1.8
- Hungary 1.5
- Ukraine 3.1
- Austria 1.7
- Belgium 1.8
- Greece 1.8
- Ireland 0.7
- Russia 4.4

- Belarus 3.7

- Luxembourg 2.3

- Netherlands 1.7

- Switzerland 1.9

The data shows that divorce rates are higher in Northern Europe and Russian Federation and lower in other parts. The EU countries with the highest divorce rates are Denmark, Sweden, Finland, and Luxembourg.

Some researchers believe that the more religious the society, the more stable the family units. For instance, Ireland and Italy, having conservative Roman Catholic beliefs, have the least divorces in Europe.

While this can be true to some extent, religion is not the critical factor influencing marriage stability. Another significant driver is the low cost of divorce in countries like Denmark and Sweden, where spouses can get divorced for roughly $100. In comparison, the cost of filing a divorce petition in the UK is around $600.

However, the low divorce costs are not the only reason for higher divorce rates. The spouses in Northern European countries are less dependent on each other financially. For example, more than 58% of Danish women aged 15-64 are employed compared to 40% in Italy and 43% in Greece, according to OECD data.

Consequently, more various employment opportunities and higher income make women less likely to stay in an unsatisfactory marriage for financial considerations.

Divorce rates in Eastern Europe (Russia, Belarus, and Ukraine) are higher than in other parts for many of the same reasons. These include the low cost of the divorce process, financial instability and poverty, and in some cases, alcoholism of one of the spouses.

Divorce Rate in Asia

Divorce rates in Asian countries have been changing in recent decades. There are a few socio-economic switches at work here, such as the increasing female educational enrollment and labor force participation.

According to research on divorce trends in Asia, other factors influencing divorce rates in this region are higher age at first marriage, changes in civil laws regulating divorce, and the extent of support for the divorced population.

The divorce rates published in the World Population Report are the following:

- Korea 2.0

- China 3.2

- Japan 1.5

- Indonesia 1.6

- Vietnam 0.2

- India 0.01

- Taiwan 2.3

- Kazakhstan 4.6

- Malaysia 1.8

- Singapore 1.7

Divorce rates vary tremendously in Asian countries, depending on their location. For example, East Asian countries (Korea, China, Japan) experience more divorces than South and East regions. Moreover, divorce rates have been growing here since 1980 and remain relatively high.

This substantial increase in divorces may be connected with a reduction social pressure to stay married and a decrease in the stigma of being divorced.

For example, if earlier South Korean men and women were less likely to get employed, these days, they have more employment opportunities and can survive divorce financially. Additionally, some East Asian societies experience a slight change towards individualism as part of the demographic transition trends.

A notable exception is Vietnam, where divorce is strongly culturally discouraged, especially in the northern and rural areas. As a result, the country's dissolution rates fell from 0.4 in 2017 to 0.23 in 2021.

The available data also shows that divorce rates in South Asia (India, Sri Lanka) are the lowest in the region. Researchers explain it by gender inequality in these countries, meaning that most women depend on their spouses and cannot return to their parents after divorce.

Divorce Rate in America

The US divorce rates have been slowly declining over the past decade. The country reached a 2.3 crude divorce rate per 1,000 in 2020, which remains the same today.

One reason for this downward trend in marriage dissolutions is fewer marriages in the first place. Another factor is that couples start getting married later in life and after reaching a certain level of financial success.

Divorce in America; Some Facts:

- The divorce rate in America is about to reach 44.2% by the end of 2022.

- Arkansas and Oklahoma show the highest number of divorces nationwide: 10.7% and 10.4%, respectively.

- Maine and the District of Columbia have the lowest divorce rates: 4.8%.

- The average length of marriage before divorce or separation is 8 years.

- Financial strain is the most commonly cited reason for divorce in the US.

- 60% of spouses married at 20-25 years old will divorce.

- The average age at first divorce in America is 30 years.

- Millennials and Gen Z have higher divorce rates - 23 and 27 divorces per 1,000 people - than other generations.

- Second marriages have a 50% divorce rate.

Divorce Rate in Africa

Africa has 57 countries, geographically divided into Northern Africa and Sub-Saharan Africa. These two regions differ in divorce rates.

Data from surveys demonstrate the following divorce rates in African countries:

- Egypt 2.2

- Algeria 1.5

- Tunisia 1.2

- Libya 0.5

- South Africa 0.4

- Ethiopia 2.6

- Kenya 0.06

- Zimbabwe 0.07

- Mozambique 0.04

The main factors influencing divorce rates in Africa are age at first marriage, financial independence, polygyny, and HIV/AIDS risks. According to research on divorce in sub-Saharan Africa, it is especially true for women, who initiate divorce more often than men.

The following statistics demonstrate the percentage of divorced women based on the abovementioned factors:

- Women with secondary school education: 34.6 %

- Women living in urban areas: 38.6%

- Women employed outside the household: 57.6%

- Women in monogamous union: 75.1%

Divorce rates in several countries are declining slowly. For example, there were 0.3 divorces for every 1,000 people in 2019 in South Africa, and now there are 0.27 divorces. This tendency can be partly attributed to the drop in marriages in the country. According to the Department of Statistics of South Africa, unions declined by 45.1% from 2011 to 2019.

The African countries with the least divorce rates are Zimbabwe, Mozambique, Kenya, South Africa, and Libya. However, the latest trends in these countries show more divorce cases. For instance, Zimbabwe has seen an increase of 234 divorces compared to 2020.

The stability of marriage in sub-Saharan African countries largely depends on religion and extended family ties. In particular, conservative Christians, who considered divorce a taboo in the past, now increasingly believe it to be a better option than domestic violence and infidelity.

In addition, if a marriage requires paying a substantial amount of money to the bride's family, maternal relatives will try to keep the union from falling apart. Otherwise, they will have to return the portion or all of the "bride price."

Divorce Rate in Latin America

Divorce rates in Latin America remain lower than in western and eastern countries. It may be attributed to the lower income and educational level of women who cannot support themselves after divorce.

For instance, only 65% of girls 11-14 years old finished secondary school, and less than 50% graduated from high school in 2019.

Divorce rates in the countries of Latin America are relatively low, according to a 2022 poll, World Population Review, and national surveys:

- Mexico 1.2
- Dominican Republic 1.2
- Costa Rica 2.3
- Cuba 2.9
- Trinidad and Tobago 2.0
- Brazil 0.4
- Peru 0.5
- Uruguay 0.9
- Guatemala 0.5
- Venezuela 0.7

- Panama 1.1

- Jamaica 1.2

The results show that divorce rates are higher in the countries located in Central America and the Caribbean compared to the countries in the south. These differences can be explained by many factors, one of which is the restriction to getting divorced in the Southern Latin region until the late 20th century.

For example, the Mexican legislature allowed dissolutions in 1914, but Brazil forbade divorces until 1977. Research explains that high divorce rates in Mexico might also be the result of the introduction of a unilateral (uncontested) divorce, making the process easier and faster.

The closer the countries are to the US border, the more divorces they have. The increase may result from a "westernization" of views on relationships and the role of women in society and the labor market, says the National Healthy Marriage Resource Center fact sheet.

South America has low marriage rates, which indirectly influences the divorce rates in the region. Moreover, unofficial unions and cohabitation are more common here than in other parts of Latin America.

Another reason for low divorce rates in Latin America is that family unity is culturally valued. It leads to couples staying together even when there is an abusive relationship.

The Impact of Divorce On Individuals and Families

Divorce can have significant impacts on both individuals and families. Some potential effects include:

1. Emotional distress: Divorce often leads to emotional turmoil, anxiety, and depression for both spouses and their children. It can be a challenging period of adjustment and coping.

2. Financial strain: Splitting assets and managing separate households can lead to financial difficulties for both parties involved, potentially affecting their standard of living.

3. Parenting challenges: Co-parenting after divorce can be complex, requiring effective communication and cooperation for the well-being of the children.
H
4. Social adjustments: Divorce can impact social circles and support networks, leading to feelings of isolation and loss.

5. Effect on children: Children may experience behavioral changes, academic difficulties, and emotional challenges as they navigate the changes in their family structure.

6. Legal and administrative burdens: Divorce proceedings involve legal processes that can be time-consuming, costly, and emotionally draining.

It's essential to remember that the impact of divorce varies from person to person and depends on various factors such as the age of the individuals involved, the reasons for the divorce, and the level of support available from family and friends. Seeking professional help, such as counseling or therapy, can often be beneficial in dealing with the challenges brought about by divorce.

Conflict Resolution

Conflict resolution refers to the process of addressing and resolving disagreements, disputes, or conflicts between individuals, groups, or organizations. It aims to find a peaceful and mutually acceptable solution to the issues at hand.

Types of Conflict: Conflicts can be interpersonal (between individuals), intragroup (within a group), intergroup (between different groups), or even intrapersonal (within an individual).

Importance of Conflict Resolution:
- Promotes healthier relationships and communication.
- Enhances team collaboration and productivity.
- Reduces negative emotions and stress.
- Can lead to innovative solutions when handled constructively.

Conflict Resolution Styles:
- Collaboration: Working together to find a solution that satisfies all parties.
- Compromise: Each side gives up something to meet in the middle.
- Competing: One party pursues their own interests without considering the other's.
- Accommodating: One party gives in to the other's desires.
- Avoiding: Ignoring or sidestepping the conflict.

Steps in Conflict Resolution:
- Identify the Issue: Clearly define the source of the conflict.
- Understand the Interests: Identify the underlying needs and motivations of each party.
- Generate Options: Brainstorm possible solutions that meet both parties' interests.
- Evaluate Options: Assess the pros and cons of each solution.
- Choose a Solution: Select the solution that best addresses the conflict.
- Implement the Solution: Put the chosen solution into action.
- Review and Adjust: After some time, evaluate the effectiveness of the solution and make adjustments if needed.

Effective Communication:

- Active listening. Truly hearing the other person's perspective.

- Nonviolent communication: Expressing feelings and needs without blame or judgment.

- I-messages: Expressing concerns using "I" statements to avoid sounding accusatory.

- Asking open-ended questions: Encouraging deeper understanding.

Emotional Intelligence:

- Recognizing and managing one's own emotions.

- Understanding and empathizing with the emotions of others.

Third-Party Mediation:

- Sometimes, conflicts may require a neutral third party to help facilitate the resolution process.

Cultural Sensitivity:

- Cultural differences can impact how conflicts are perceived and resolved.

Practice and Patience:

- Conflict resolution skills improve over time with practice and patience.

Remember, conflict resolution is about finding common ground and fostering understanding, rather than "winning" a dispute. It involves respectful communication, empathy, and a willingness to collaborate towards a mutually beneficial outcome. You and your spouse should inculcate the habit of empathy towards each other; listening and understanding from each other's point of view.

How To Improve Your Conflict Resolution Skills

Improving your conflict resolution skills takes practice and self-awareness. Here are some steps you can take to enhance your abilities in this area:

1. Self-Reflection: Take some time to think about how you currently handle conflicts. Identify your strengths and areas for improvement.

2. Active Listening: Practice active listening by fully focusing on what the other person is saying without interrupting. This helps you understand their perspective better.

3. Empathy: Put yourself in the other person's shoes and try to understand their feelings and needs. Empathy can foster a more open and understanding atmosphere.

4. Effective Communication: Work on expressing yourself clearly and calmly. Use "I" statements to express your feelings without blaming or accusing.

5. Stay Calm: Develop techniques to manage your own emotions during conflicts. Deep breathing or taking a short break can help you stay composed.

6. Problem-Solving Skills: Practice brainstorming solutions to conflicts. Think creatively and encourage open discussion of different options.

7. Mediation and Negotiation: Learn about mediation techniques and negotiation skills. These can help you facilitate resolutions between conflicting parties.

8. Conflict Scenarios: Role-play different conflict scenarios with a friend or colleague. This practice can help you refine your approach and try out different strategies.

9. Learn from Experience: After resolving a conflict, take time to reflect on what worked well and what could be improved for next time.

10. Seek Feedback: Ask for feedback from trusted friends, family members, or colleagues on your conflict resolution skills. This can provide valuable insights.

11. Conflict Resolution Training: Consider attending workshops, courses, or seminars focused on conflict resolution. These can provide you with structured learning and practical techniques.

12. Read and Learn: There are numerous books, articles, and online resources that delve into conflict resolution strategies. Learning from experts in the field can offer valuable insights.

13. Practice Patience: Conflict resolution can take time. Be patient and persistent in finding solutions that satisfy all parties involved.

14. Apply Skills Regularly: Look for opportunities to apply your conflict resolution skills in everyday situations. The more you practice, the more natural these skills will become.

Remember that conflict resolution is an ongoing journey, and improvement takes time. Be open to learning, adapting, and growing in your ability to handle conflicts constructively.

Example Of Active Listening

Certainly! Active listening is a crucial skill in conflict resolution. Here's an example of how active listening might look in a conversation:

Person A: "I've been feeling really overwhelmed with all the tasks I have to complete at work. I just can't seem to keep up."

Person B (practising active listening): "It sounds like you're feeling quite overwhelmed with your workload. Can you tell me more about the specific tasks that are causing you stress?"

In this example, Person B is actively listening by paraphrasing and reflecting back what Person A said. They also ask an open-ended question to encourage Person A to share more details. This approach shows that Person B is genuinely interested in understanding Person A's feelings and experiences, creating a supportive environment for communication.

Active listening involves not only hearing the words but also understanding the emotions and context behind them. It helps to build rapport, demonstrate empathy, and promote a deeper understanding of the speaker's perspective.

Active listening is a communication skill that involves fully concentrating, understanding, responding, and remembering what the speaker is saying. It goes beyond just hearing the words and involves engaging with the speaker to comprehend their message, emotions, and underlying meaning. Here are some key aspects of active listening:

1. Engagement: Active listening requires your full attention. Put away distractions like your phone or other tasks and focus solely on the speaker.

2. Nonverbal Cues: Use positive body language, such as making eye contact, nodding, and facing the speaker. These gestures show that you are engaged and interested.

3. Paraphrasing: Summarize or rephrase what the speaker said to show that you understand and to clarify any misunderstandings. This also demonstrates that you're actively processing the information.

4. Reflecting Feelings: Pay attention to the speaker's emotions and reflect them back. For example, "It seems like you're frustrated because of the situation."

5. Asking Open-Ended Questions: Encourage the speaker to elaborate and share more by asking questions that can't be answered with a simple "yes" or "no."

6. Empathy: Put yourself in the speaker's shoes and try to understand their perspective. Show genuine concern for their feelings and experiences.

7. Avoid Interrupting: Allow the speaker to finish their thoughts before responding. Interrupting can hinder the flow of their communication and might make them feel unheard.

8. Minimal Encouragers: Use short verbal cues like "I see," "Go on," or "Tell me more" to show that you're engaged and interested in hearing more.

9. Withhold Judgment: Suspend your own opinions or judgments while the speaker is talking. This helps create an open and safe space for them to express themselves.

10. Provide Feedback: Once the speaker has finished, offer feedback that demonstrates your understanding and validates their feelings. This could involve summarizing what they said or expressing empathy.

Active listening is an essential skill not only for conflict resolution but also for effective communication in general. It builds trust, encourages open dialogue, and can lead to better understanding and collaboration between individuals.

Conflict Resolutions In Various Scenarios

1. Workplace Conflict
   Situation: Two colleagues have differing opinions about how a project should be approached.
   Resolution: They schedule a meeting to discuss their ideas openly, listen to each other's perspectives, and then collaboratively come up with a hybrid approach that incorporates both viewpoints.

2. Family Conflict
   Situation: Siblings are arguing over who gets to use the computer first.
   Resolution: The parents mediate the situation by suggesting a fair schedule for computer usage, considering each sibling's needs and responsibilities.

3. Neighbor Dispute

Situation: Neighbors are arguing over the height of a shared fence that blocks sunlight.

Resolution: They engage in a calm conversation, considering local regulations and each other's concerns, and agree on a compromise height for the fence that allows both parties to benefit.

4. Team Project Conflict

Situation: Members of a project team are disagreeing about the best approach to meet a tight deadline.

Resolution: The team leader calls a meeting where everyone can share their thoughts. They work together to identify the most efficient tasks for each member, ensuring the project is completed on time.

5. Friendship Conflict

Situation: Two friends are upset with each other after a misunderstanding about plans.

Resolution: They meet up to talk it out, actively listen to each other's explanations, and apologize for any miscommunication. They clarify their intentions and reaffirm their friendship.

6. Parent-Child Conflict

Situation: A teenager wants to attend a party, but their parents are concerned about safety and curfew.

Resolution: The family holds a family meeting where they discuss the teenager's desire to attend the party. The parents express their concerns, and the teenager proposes compromises such as checking in periodically during the party and adhering to the curfew.

7. Business Partnership Conflict

Situation: Business partners disagree on the allocation of profits and decision-making authority.

Resolution: They hire a professional mediator to facilitate discussions and help them come to an agreement on profit sharing and decision-making responsibilities that both partners find acceptable.

8. Online Community Conflict

Situation: Users on an online forum are arguing over differing opinions on a topic.

Resolution: A moderator steps in to remind everyone of the forum's rules and guidelines for respectful communication. They encourage users to focus on constructive debate and avoid personal attacks.

These examples showcase how conflict resolution involves effective communication, empathy, active listening, and finding common ground to reach a solution that satisfies all parties involved.

Training Options For Conflict Resolutions

There are various conflict resolution training options available, ranging from online courses to workshops and certifications. Here are some options you might consider:

1. Online Courses

Coursera: Offers courses on conflict resolution, negotiation skills, and communication.

Udemy: Provides a range of conflict resolution courses suitable for different skill levels.

LinkedIn Learning: Offers video courses on conflict management, communication, and emotional intelligence.

2. Local Workshops and Seminars:

- Check with local community centers, universities, or professional organizations for workshops on conflict resolution and communication skills.

3. University or College Programs:

- Some universities offer degree programs or courses related to conflict resolution, mediation, or negotiation.

4. Professional Associations:

- Organizations like the Association for Conflict Resolution (ACR) and the International Mediation Institute (IMI) often offer training and resources.

5. Mediation Training Centers:

- Look for organizations that specialize in mediation and conflict resolution training. They often offer comprehensive programs for individuals interested in becoming professional mediators.

6. Corporate Training Programs:

- Many companies offer conflict resolution and communication training as part of employee development programs.

7. Nonprofit Organizations:

- Organizations focused on peacebuilding, community development, and social justice might offer conflict resolution workshops and training.

8. Books and Resources:

- There are numerous books on conflict resolution techniques and strategies. Look for titles by authors like Dale Carnegie, Roger Fisher, and William Ury.

9. Online Webinars and Seminars:

- Many experts in conflict resolution offer webinars and virtual seminars on various aspects of the topic.

10. Government Agencies and NGOs:

- Some government departments and nonprofit organizations provide conflict resolution training for specific fields, such as education, healthcare, and community development.

When choosing a training option, consider factors such as your current level of expertise, your learning preferences (online, in-person, or a combination), and your specific goals for improving your conflict resolution skills. Additionally, read reviews and testimonials to ensure the training is reputable and aligns with your needs.

Handling conflicts involving emotions requires a sensitive and empathetic approach. Here are some steps to navigate emotionally charged conflicts:

1. Stay Calm Yourself: Emotional conflicts can escalate quickly if both parties are upset. Stay composed to model a calm and respectful tone.

2. Give Space and Time: If emotions are running high, consider taking a break to allow everyone to cool down before continuing the discussio.

3. **Acknowledge Emotions: Recognize and validate the emotions of all parties involved. This helps them feel heard and understood.

4. Listen Actively: Pay close attention to what each person is saying, as well as the emotions underlying their words.

5. Use "I" Statements: Express your thoughts and feelings using "I" statements to avoid sounding accusatory. For example, "I feel hurt when..." instead of "You always..."

6. Empathize: Show understanding and empathy for how the other person is feeling. Use phrases like "I can see why you might feel that way."

7. Address Emotions First: Sometimes, it's helpful to address the emotional aspect of the conflict before diving into the practical issues. This can help create a more open atmosphere for discussion.

8. Focus on Common Goals: Remind everyone of the shared goals or interests that can help guide the resolution process.

9. Clarify Misunderstandings: Often, emotions arise from misunderstandings. Take time to clarify points of confusion and ensure everyone is on the same page.

10. Use Reflective Listening: Repeat back what you hear from the other person to show that you're actively listening and understanding their feelings.

11. Use Positive Language: Frame your responses in a positive manner, highlighting areas of agreement or common ground.

12. Avoid Blame and Accusations: Keep the conversation focused on the issues and emotions rather than assigning blame.

13. Seek Solutions Together: Collaborate on finding solutions that address both the emotional concerns and the practical issues at hand.

14. Apologize If Necessary: If your actions contributed to the emotional conflict, apologize sincerely.

15. Focus on Future Solutions: While acknowledging emotions, shift the focus towards finding ways to prevent similar conflicts in the future.

16. Consider Mediation: If emotions are particularly intense, consider involving a neutral third party to mediate the conversation and ensure a productive outcome.

Remember, conflicts involving emotions require patience, empathy, and a willingness to understand the emotional factors driving the conflict. Taking the time to address emotions can pave the way for a more productive and satisfying resolution.

Techniques That Enhances Effective Listening

Several techniques can enhance your active listening skills, making your conversations more effective and meaningful. Here are some techniques to consider:

1. Maintain Eye Contact: Sustaining appropriate eye contact shows that you're engaged and attentive to the speaker.

2. Use Open Body Language: Keep your posture open and relaxed, signaling that you're approachable and interested.

3. Avoid Interrupting: Let the speaker finish their thoughts before responding. Interrupting can disrupt their flow and hinder understanding.

4. Nod and Provide Feedback: Nodding occasionally and using verbal cues like "I see," "Go on," or "Interesting" indicates that you're actively following the conversation.

5. Minimal Encouragers: Use short responses like "Yes," "I understand," or "Tell me more" to encourage the speaker to continue sharing.

6. Paraphrasing: Repeat back what you've heard in your own words. This demonstrates that you're processing the information and ensures you understood correctly.

7. Reflecting Feelings: Acknowledge the speaker's emotions by saying things like "It sounds like you're feeling frustrated about this situation."

8. Asking Open-Ended Questions: Pose questions that can't be answered with a simple "yes" or "no." This encourages the speaker to elaborate and share more details.

9. Empathize: Express understanding and empathy by saying phrases like "I can imagine how that must have been tough."

10. Avoid Distractions: Put away your phone or other distractions so you can give your full attention to the conversation.

11. Focus on the Speaker: Concentrate on the speaker's words, tone, and nonverbal cues. Avoid mentally preparing your response while they're talking.

12. Summarize and Recap: Periodically summarize what you've heard to ensure you're on the same page and to help the speaker organize their thoughts.

13. Practice Active Pause: Use brief pauses before responding to ensure the speaker has finished and to give you time to process their message.

14. Practice Empathetic Listening: Try to understand the emotions and motivations behind the speaker's words. Put yourself in their shoes.

15. Limit Judgments and Assumptions: Avoid making judgments or assumptions about the speaker's intentions. Listen with an open mind.

16. Take Notes (if appropriate): In some contexts, taking notes can help you remember key points and show your commitment to the conversation.

17. Be Patient: Allow the speaker to express themselves fully, even if they take a bit of time to articulate their thoughts.

Active listening involves being fully present, attentive, and responsive in a conversation. By practicing these techniques, you can strengthen your ability to understand others and build better relationships.

Reflective Listening

Practicing reflective listening can greatly enhance your communication and empathy skills. Here's how you can practice reflective listening:

1. Choose the Right Setting: Find a quiet and comfortable environment where you won't be interrupted.

2. Select a Partner: Choose someone you trust and feel comfortable with. This could be a friend, family member, or colleague.

3. Be Present: Put away distractions and focus solely on the speaker.

4. Listen Actively: Pay close attention to the speaker's words, tone, and nonverbal cues.

5. Paraphrase: After the speaker has shared their thoughts, repeat back what you heard using your own words. Try to capture the main points of their message.

6. Avoid Exact Repetition: Instead of repeating their words verbatim, aim to convey the essence of what they said.

7. Use Open-Ended Statements: Start your reflection with statements like "It sounds like..." or "If I understand correctly...".

8. Clarify and Confirm: Ask the speaker if your reflection is accurate. This shows that you genuinely want to understand them correctly.

9. Reflect Emotions: If the speaker expresses emotions, reflect those feelings back in your paraphrase. For example, "It sounds like you're feeling frustrated because..."

10. Wait for Confirmation: Allow the speaker to confirm whether your reflection accurately captures their thoughts and feelings.

11. Be Patient: If the speaker corrects or adds more information, be patient and adjust your reflection accordingly.

12. Ask for More Details: If there are aspects you're not clear about, ask for more details to ensure you fully understand.

13. Practice Active Listening Skills: Use techniques like nodding, maintaining eye contact, and using minimal encouragers while reflecting.

14. Offer Positive Feedback: Let the speaker know that you value their perspective and appreciate their openness.

15. Rotate Roles: After practicing reflective listening, switch roles with your partner so both of you have a chance to practice speaking and listening.

16. Reflect on Your Experience: After the practice session, reflect on how well you were able to capture the speaker's message and emotions. Consider areas for improvement.

Remember that reflective listening is a skill that develops with practice. It helps to approach it with a genuine desire to understand and empathize with the speaker's perspective. Over time, practicing reflective listening can strengthen your communication skills and improve your relationships.

Varying Examples of Conflict Resolutions

Scenario: Two team members, Alex and Taylor, have been assigned to collaborate on a project. However, they've been experiencing conflicts due to differences in work styles and communication.

Conflict Resolution:

1. Initiating the Conversation:
   - Team Leader: Notices the tension and schedules a private meeting with Alex and Taylor.

2. Active Listening and Empathy:

   - Team Leader (to Alex and Taylor): "I've noticed that there have been some challenges in your collaboration. Could you each share your perspective on what's been happening?"

3. Sharing Perspectives:

   - Alex: "I feel like Taylor doesn't communicate enough and doesn't give me enough information to work effectively."

   - Taylor: "I've been focusing on getting things done efficiently, but I can see how my approach might come across as dismissive."

4. Validating Emotions:

   - Team Leader: "It sounds like both of you have valid concerns. Alex, you want clearer communication, and Taylor, you're trying to streamline the process."

5. Identifying Common Ground:

   - Team Leader: "Both of you want the project to succeed. Let's find a way to work together that addresses both your needs."

6. Brainstorming Solutions:

   - Alex: "Maybe we could have regular check-ins to discuss progress and clarify any questions."

   - Taylor: "That could work, and I'll make sure to provide more context in my communications."

7. Agreeing on a Resolution:

   - Team Leader: "It sounds like you're agreeing on having regular check-ins and improving communication. Let's make sure you both feel comfortable with this solution."

8. Implementation:

- Alex and Taylor: Start scheduling regular check-ins and adapting their communication styles to better align.

9. Feedback and Follow-Up:
  - Team Leader: After a few weeks, checks in with Alex and Taylor to see how the new approach is working. Provides positive feedback for their efforts.

In this example, the conflict was addressed by facilitating a conversation where both parties shared their perspectives. The team leader ensured that emotions were validated and that both individuals felt heard. A solution was agreed upon, and the progress was followed up to ensure the resolution was effective. This approach demonstrates active listening, empathy, and a collaborative attitude toward finding common ground.

Conclusion

Navigating Marriage and Divorce with Understanding and Resilience

In the journey of exploring marriage and divorce, we have delved into the intricate web of human relationships, emotions, and life-altering decisions. Throughout this book, we have come to realize that marriage is a profound commitment that carries with it moments of joy, challenges, growth, and sometimes, the painful reality of divorce. As we conclude our exploration, several overarching themes emerge that shed light on how we can navigate these complex pathways with empathy, understanding, and resilience.

Marriage, as we have learned, is a partnership that demands open communication, active listening, and continuous effort. It is built on a foundation of mutual respect, trust, and shared values. While the journey is not without its hurdles, the stories and advice shared within these pages remind us that the challenges can be overcome when both partners approach them with a willingness to learn and adapt.

Inevitably, discussions of marriage lead us to the topic of divorce, a topic that is often shrouded in stigma and heartache. We have gained insight into the multifaceted reasons behind divorce, from irreconcilable differences to personal growth that takes divergent paths. What stands out is the importance of recognizing that divorce is not a sign of failure but can be an act of courage and self-preservation. The experiences shared here emphasize that, even in the face of separation, respectful communication and empathy can help both parties navigate the process and, if needed, co-parent effectively.

As we move forward, let us remember that the wisdom of learning from both successes and struggles can guide us towards healthier relationships, whether they be marriages built on love and commitment or the paths to healing that arise from divorce.

Ultimately, this book is a reminder that life's journey is not always linear. It takes unexpected turns, presents unforeseen challenges, and offers moments of immense joy. Whether in the embrace of a lasting marriage or in the process of rebuilding after divorce, what truly matters is the empathy we show ourselves and others. May the stories and insights within these pages serve as guiding lights, encouraging us all to approach the complexities of marriage and divorce with compassion, understanding, and an unwavering commitment to our own well-being and growth.

To your marriage success.

Shirley A. Wass.